Where the Flame Trees Bloom

by Alma Flor Ada

illustrated by Antonio Martorell

Atheneum Books for Young Readers

To Samantha Rose
as your life begins to bloom
—A. F. A.

Except for the three stories *Rag Dolls*, *Mathematics*, and *The Surveyor*, which
were written in English, the stories in this volume were first written in Spanish.
The author would like to thank her daughter, Rosa Zubizarreta, for her fine
translations of those stories as well as for her sharp editorial eye and advice
on the others.

Text copyright © 1994 by Alma Flor Ada
Illustrations copyright © 1994 by Antonio Martorell

Atheneum Books for Young Readers
An imprint of Simon & Schuster Children's Publishing Division
1230 Avenue of the Americas, New York, New York 10020

All rights reserved including the right of reproduction in whole or in part in any form.

Manufactured in China
10 9 8 7 6 5 4

The text of this book is set in Bembo.
Book design by Laura Hammond Hough.

Library of Congress Catalog Card Number: 94-071876
ISBN 1-4169-6840-7 ISBN 978-1-4169-6840-5

CENTRAL ARKANSAS LIBRARY SYSTEM
ROOSEVELT L. THOMPSON BRANCH LIBRARY
LITTLE ROCK, ARKANSAS

Contents

∞

Introduction

I was born in Cuba. The largest of the islands in the Caribbean, Cuba is long and narrow. If one looks at a map of Cuba with a little bit of imagination, the island resembles a giant alligator, resting on the water. The western part of Cuba is very close to Florida, while the eastern part is very close to the Dominican Republic and Haiti. In climate and natural beauty, Cuba is very similar to Puerto Rico. In fact, Cubans and Puerto Ricans have a shared history, which is why a Puerto Rican poet once said that "Cuba and Puerto Rico are two wings of the same bird."

On both ends and in the center, Cuba has high mountain ranges covered with dense tropical forests. In between these three mountainous regions there are flat, fertile lands. I grew up in the eastern plains, the cattle region, on the outskirts of Camagüey, a town of brick houses with tile roofs, and strong old churches built of stone, which in the past had served as both houses of worship and refuges from pirates. The churches' high towers once allowed lookouts to keep watch for cattle-thieving buccaneers.

The house I was born in was very large and very old. My great-grandfather on my mother's side had given it to my grandmother, his daughter. My youngest aunt, Lolita, had been born in the house. A generation later two of my cousins, my younger sister Flor, and myself were also born in the same house.

Although the house was large, we were not wealthy. However, I did grow up surrounded by a wealth of family. At one time or another, grandparents, aunts, uncles, and cousins all lived together under that roof. Yet for the first seven years of my childhood I was the only child living in the house. Two older cousins came occasionally for visits.

The house we lived in held a lot of history too. It had been built as a colonial *hacienda* for an Italian family, the Simoni. In the hacienda they planted crops, raised cattle, tanned hides, and made bricks, tiles, and household vessels from the red clay found by the river. In those days, all the work was done by the people the Simoni kept as slaves.

Much later, by the time I was a child, the house had grown old and weathered. The gardens were overgrown. And the fountain, dry and filled with earth, served as a planter for ferns. Behind the house still stood the slave quarters. And the remains of a dungeon, the *calabozo,* were proof of the horrible things human beings can do to each other. Once upon a time slaves had been chained to the iron rings on its walls.

During the colonial times, one of the two daughters of the Simoni family, Amelia, married Ignacio Agramonte, one of the Cuban patriots who fought to gain independence and freedom for all who lived in Cuba. One of the first acts of the Cuban Revolution in 1868 was to free all slaves.

It was this connection with the Cuban struggle for freedom, not its earlier history, that made my family proud of our home. For me, the past was still filled with unexplainable questions: How could anyone dare to think that he could own or control anyone else? And why were we so proud of freedom and independence while some children walked the countryside barefoot and hungry?

Despite these questions—big ones for the child I was—the old house was for me a magic world all the same. My grandmother kept large flocks of chickens, ducks, and geese, and as a reflection of her love of beauty, peacocks as well. The peacocks would often perch in the dining room windows, which opened out into a garden. Sometimes they would nest atop a large white masonry arch, which had been built long before as a small-scale replica of the French Arc de Triomphe in the now abandoned garden by the river. Bats lived in the eaves under the porch, and doves lived on the terrace. My mother took in every lost cat that crossed her path, and the garden was busy with lizards, snails, frogs and toads, and crickets and grasshoppers. Hidden in the branches of a nearby tree lived a family of hawks; but among all these living things my best friends were the trees.

Big, firm, and strong, they offered me their friendship in many ways. Their green canopies created a treasured shade during the heat of the day, allowing me to stay outdoors, protected from the tropical sun. Whether I was lonely or joyful, they always welcomed me.

Flame trees, more than a hundred years old, formed an avenue along one side of the house leading to the white arch and the river. They were gnarled with age. Their large roots protruded from the earth, offering me a nest where I could crawl in and feel protected and secure. The roots, worn smooth by the weather, were soft to the touch, and I would caress them as one would hold a friend's hand.

The old river, winding its way through the land, had formed a rather large island behind the house. Long ago the island had been planted with fruit trees. Now the mature trees were generous with their fruit, offering throughout the year different surprises far better than any dessert coming from our kitchen or any candy that could be bought at the store. Bittersweet *marañones,* looking like bright bells, strikingly yellow or deeply red, each one with its delicious nut hanging below: the cashew nuts that my uncle Medardito and my younger aunt Lolita loved to roast on a campfire by the river; sweet and sour *tamarindos,* which we would soak in water to make a delicious drink; fragrant *guayabas,* brilliantly green outside and a sweet red inside; *caimitos,* round as a baseball, with shining purple skin and delicate milky white flesh. And then there were dozens of coconut trees, whose fruit, the *cocos,* we treasured above all. They swayed with the wind making the island always fresh and breezy. The water of the young coconuts is fresh and sweet. As the young coconut matures, the water inside slowly becomes more solid, smooth as a light gelatin. We loved to eat them as they became fleshier but were still soft and sweet. When the coconut meat became hard and dry, it was used to make desserts. And finally there was the most highly valued and hardest to find. If a large, healthy coconut was kept for several weeks, perhaps even several months, at the right temperature, in a moist and shadowy place, then perhaps it would sprout. And if it did, and someone knew how to open it at the right time, she would find that the thick, dry meat inside the coconut had pulled away from the husk and had gathered in the center of the coconut as a soft, porous ball, the *"manzana del coco"* or "apple of the coconut," exquisitely sweet.

On one of the island's shores stood a bamboo grove where my grandmother would hang her hammock every afternoon, to rest for a while between her two jobs, as the principal of a school for children in the morning and a school for women at night. The rustle of the bamboos and the coconut palms provided an enchanting, soothing melody. Although we lived far inland, a couple of hours away from the ocean shore, the sea breezes seemed still to share rumors of distant lands and remote places.

Though I grew up surrounded by loving people and fascinated by all the life around me, it was to the trees that I told my sorrows and my joys, and especially my dreams.

It was the trees that, like a family, grew and branched out. Like all of life, they yielded in some ways to stories that came and went. Some, like the flame trees, were stolid and almost timeless. Others were abundant with fruit and offspring. I could not help but see how in their own way, they described the life around me—life that is reflected in these stories I will tell.

The stories of my family all took place at various times. Some happened before I was born and were told to me as a child. The others all happened as I was growing up, until I was about ten years old. Most of them took place in the magnificent old house, the Quinta Simoni where I lived until I was eight. In others you will see more of the town itself, where we moved after that. But even in town I was fortunately never too far from the generous trees majestically swaying in the tropical breezes, or, as with the flame trees, bursting with fiery red flowers… blossoming… blossoming… blossoming.

As I share these stories with you, I can still see the tall and majestic royal palms, the coconut trees swaying easily in the warm tropical breezes, and the fiery flame trees, bursting all over with their abundant red blossoms. And I hope that the inspiration that I continue to receive from these companions of my childhood will, in turn, help warm the hearts of others.

The Teacher

∞

My mother's mother, my grandmother Dolores, was known as Lola. She filled my early years with outdoor adventures, fun, and fascinating stories. The deeds of the Greek gods and goddesses, the heroic feats of the Cuban patriots, were as immediate to me as her everyday life at the two schools where she was principal: an elementary public school during the day and a school for working women in the evenings.

It is not surprising that there are many stories in our family about this woman who was both an intellectual and a practical person, who cut her hair and shortened her skirts before any other woman in our town, who created a literary journal, founded schools, awakened a great passion in the poet who married her, and brought up five children as well as several nieces and nephews while directing her own schools and farm.

One of my favorite stories about her was told to me at various times by my mother and by my aunts Mireya and Virginia, since all three of them were present when the events took place. Unlike many other family stories, which are often changed or embellished depending on the teller, I have always heard this story told exactly the same way. Perhaps that is because the story itself is too powerful to be embellished, or because the events impressed themselves so vividly upon the memories of those present.

My grandmother Lola loved to teach outdoors. The slightest pretext would serve to take the whole class out under the trees to conduct her lessons there. This particular story took place during one of those outdoor lessons, at a time when she and her husband, my grandfather Medardo, ran a boarding school on the hacienda she had inherited from her father and where later I would be born.

Surrounded by her pupils, including three of her own daughters, my grandmother was conducting a grammar lesson. Suddenly she interrupted herself. "Why is it," she asked her students, "that we don't often speak about the things that are truly important? About our responsibility as human beings for those around us? Do we really know their feelings, their needs? And yet we could all do so much for each other. . . ."

The students were silent, spellbound. They knew their teacher sometimes strayed from the topic of the lesson in order to share with them her own reflections. And they also knew that those were some of her most important lessons. At times she could be funny and witty. Other times, she would touch their hearts. And so they listened.

"Look," continued my grandmother, as she pointed to the road that bordered the farm. There the students saw a solitary man walking. "Look at that old man. He is walking by us. In a few minutes he will be gone forever, and we will never have known who he is, where he is going, what may be important in his life."

The students watched the man, who by then was quite close. He was very thin, and a coarse *guayabera* hung loosely over his bent frame. His face, in the shade of a straw hat, was weathered and wrinkled.

"Well," said my grandmother, "do we let him go away, forever unknown, or do you want to ask him if there is anything we can do for him?"

The students looked at one another. Finally one girl said: "Shall I ask him?" As my grandmother nodded, the girl got up and walked toward the road. A few of the other students followed her, my mother and my aunts among them.

Upon seeing them approach, the man stopped. "We would like to know who you are, and where you are going," said the student. "Is there anything we can do for you?" added my aunt Mireya.

The man was completely taken aback. "But, who are *you*?" was all he could reply.

The girls then explained how their questions had come about. The old man looked at them. He told them that he had no one to be with, that he had come a long distance hoping to find some distant relatives, but had been unable to locate them. "I'm nothing but an old man," he concluded, "looking for a place to lie down and die. As a matter of fact, I was heading toward that large *ceiba*." He pointed to a large tree growing by the road not too far away. "I thought I'd lie down in its shade to wait for my death."

"Please don't leave" was all the girls could say. They rushed back to tell their teacher what they had learned from the old man, that he truly intended to just lie down and die.

"What do you think can be done?" my grandmother asked. The boys and girls came up with ideas: The old man could go to an old folks' home. Maybe he should be taken to the hospital, or perhaps the police would know what to do. . . . "Is that what you would like to happen, if it were you?" my grandmother asked.

Instead, the children took the man into the house. He was given a room. The students made the bed and cooked him some food. A doctor determined that there was nothing wrong with him except exhaustion and malnutrition. It took him several days to recuperate, but soon he was up and about. He lived on with the family for many years, until one morning he was found to have died peacefully in his sleep. During all those years, he helped in the garden, fed the hens, or often sat on the back porch, whistling softly. But there was nothing he liked better than to sit in the back of the classroom or out under the trees and listen to my grandmother teach.

Choices

My father's family and my mother's family were as different from each other as a quiet mountain stream and the vast ocean. My father's family was small in contrast to my mother's, with its many aunts, uncles, first and second cousins, great-aunts, and great-uncles. But not only was my mother's family large, it also was very lively, cheerful, and adventurous, while my father's father and brothers were quiet people who seldom spoke about anything personal.

We frequently spent our evenings together listening to stories of my mother's family. Through these stories people whom I had never met seemed as familiar to me as those who lived nearby. It seemed as though I had heard their voices and taken part in their adventures. But it is a story told to me by my father's father that I would like to share with you now, a story that remains vivid in my memory and that has greatly shaped who I am today.

My grandfather Modesto would stop by my house every afternoon for a short visit, always with a cigarette between his yellowed fingers. He would pat me on the head or give me a formal kiss on the forehead, and then he would sit and talk with my parents about the political and social issues of the day. He sounded very knowledgeable to me, but also adult and remote. He was a large, formidable man, and although I listened in fascination to his words, I felt as if it would be many years before I would be able to share anything with him, or he with me.

One afternoon when he arrived, my parents had gone out and I was the only one at home. He sat to wait for them in the dining room, the coolest room in the city house where we then lived. The house was bathed in the quiet so prevalent in the tropics during the hottest part of the day. As usual, I was buried in a book. Then my grandfather Modesto called my name and motioned for me to sit on his lap. I was surprised by this gesture of warmth and affection since I was almost ten years old and especially since he never asked any of us to sit by him. Yet I welcomed the invitation to get close to this man who seemed so remote and yet so wise. I never knew what prompted him to tell me the story that came next, but I have always treasured it.

"You probably know that I was once very wealthy," he began. As I nodded, he continued. "I was only twelve years old when I left Spain to come to Cuba. My father had died, and since my oldest brother was arrogant and mean, I decided to leave my home at La Coruña. I roamed the port until someone pointed out a ship that was about to sail, and I managed to hide aboard. A sailor discovered me shortly after the ship set sail, but the captain said I should sail with them, and when we arrived at Havana he helped me get ashore. I searched for work, and fortunately I was taken in by the owner of a hardware store. He worked me hard! I cleaned the store and helped with all kinds of odd jobs. I had to sleep in the storage room on some burlap sacks, but I learned the business well.

"One day a young American came into the store with a surprising machine that played music from round black disks. It was made in the United States and was called a gramophone. I was astonished and excited. Imagine, a machine that could bring the great opera singer Enrico Caruso's voice into each home! I made arrangements with this man and set out to sell this new invention. Eventually I became the major representative in Cuba for RCA, the manufacturer, and traveled the island from end to end. I loved the land around Camagüey, and I saw how cattle could thrive on these fertile plains, so I bought some land. The land turned out to be even more valuable than I thought, and I became rich."

He paused. Even though I didn't know then the

meaning of the word *nostalgia*, I know now that is exactly what I saw in his eyes. "The years passed," he continued. "I married your grandmother and we had four sons. Then, she became very ill. Since she was too ill to be moved, I had a doctor come to the hacienda. But although he did all he could, she did not improve.

"One evening, an exhausted horse and rider galloped up to the hacienda. The rider was my business manager in Havana. He'd ridden at top speed from the train station in Camagüey, and close up, I saw that it was not only exhaustion that marked his face, but panic. 'You must come to Havana immediately,' he urged me. 'There is a financial crisis and the economy is collapsing. The president of your bank sent me to warn you. It's urgent that you travel to the capital in person to withdraw all of your money or else it will be lost.' I considered his alarming news as the man looked at me impatiently, unable to understand why I wasn't ordering fresh horses to take us to the train. But was I to leave your ill grandmother?"

He paused again, and I saw that the look in his eyes had changed. This new feeling was one I recognized even as a child. My own eyes must have looked the same the day I found a bird, which only a short while ago had been alive, lying dead in our backyard.

My grandfather finished his story: "I did not return with him. Your grandmother did not get well, and the economy did collapse before I could get my money from the bank. I was no longer a rich man. But I was there by

18

your grandmother's side until the end, and I held her hand in mine as she passed away." I looked down at my grandfather's big hand, which was covering my own. And then I knew I would not have to wait until I grew up to understand my grandfather Modesto.

There is no one alive today who remembers María Rey Paz, the grandmother I never knew. And there are probably very few people living who remember my quiet but steadfast grandfather, Modesto. Yet, I am certain that these ancestors of mine live on in my children, who have known from a young age what choices to make when loved ones are concerned.

The Surveyor

∞

My father, named Modesto after my grandfather, was a surveyor. Some of the happiest
times of my childhood were spent on horseback, on trips
where he would allow me to accompany him as he plotted
the boundaries of small farms in the Cuban countryside.
Sometimes we slept out under the stars, stringing our
hammocks between the trees, and drank fresh water from
springs. We always stopped for a warm greeting at the
simple huts of the neighboring peasants, and my eyes
would drink in the lush green forest crowned by the swaying leaves of the palm trees.

Since many surveying jobs called for dividing up
land that a family had inherited from a deceased parent or
relative, my father's greatest concern was that justice be
achieved. It was not enough just to divide the land into

equal portions. He also had to ensure that all parties would have access to roads, to water sources, to the most fertile soil. While I was able to join him in some trips, other surveying work involved large areas of land. On these jobs, my father was part of a team, and I would stay home, eagerly awaiting to hear the stories from his trip on his return.

Latin American families tend not to limit their family boundaries to those who are born or have married into it. Any good friend who spends time with the family and shares in its daily experiences is welcomed as a member. The following story from one of my father's surveying trips is not about a member of my blood family, but instead concerns a member of our extended family.

Félix Caballero, a man my father always liked to recruit whenever he needed a team, was rather different from the other surveyors. He was somewhat older, unmarried, and he kept his thoughts to himself. He came to visit our house daily. Once there, he would sit silently in one of the living room's four rocking chairs, listening to the lively conversations all around him. An occasional nod or a single word were his only contributions to those conversations. My mother and her sisters sometimes made fun of him behind his back. Even though they never said so, I had the impression that they questioned why my father held him in such high regard.

Then one day my father shared this story.

"We had been working on foot in mountainous

country for most of the day. Night was approaching. We still had a long way to go to return to where we had left the horses, so we decided to cut across to the other side of the mountain, and soon found ourselves facing a deep gorge. The gorge was spanned by a railroad bridge, long and narrow, built for the sugarcane trains. There were no side rails or walkways, only a set of tracks resting on thick, heavy crossties suspended high in the air.

"We were all upset about having to climb down the steep gorge and up the other side, but the simpler solution, walking across the bridge, seemed too dangerous. What if a cane train should appear? There would be nowhere to go. So we all began the long descent . . . all except for Félix. He decided to risk walking across the railroad bridge. We all tried to dissuade him, but to no avail. Using an old method, he put one ear to the tracks to listen for vibrations. Since he heard none, he decided that no train was approaching. So he began to cross the long bridge, stepping from crosstie to crosstie between the rails, balancing his long red-and-white surveyor's poles on his shoulder.

"He was about halfway across the bridge when we heard the ominous sound of a steam engine. All eyes rose to Félix. Unquestionably he had heard it too, because he had stopped in the middle of the bridge and was looking back.

"As the train drew closer, and thinking there was no other solution, we all shouted: 'Jump! Jump!', not even sure our voices would carry up to where he stood, so high above us. Félix did look down at the rocky riverbed, which, as it was the dry season, held little water. We tried to encourage him with gestures and more shouts, but he had stopped looking down. We could not imagine what he was doing next, squatting on the tracks, with the engine of the train already visible. And then, we understood. . . .

"Knowing that he could not manage to hold on to the thick wooden crossties, Félix laid his thin but resilient surveyor's poles across the ties, parallel to the rails. Then he let his body slip down between two of the ties, as he held on to the poles. And there he hung, below the bridge, suspended over the gorge but safely out of the train's path.

"The cane train was, as they frequently are, a very long train. To us, it seemed interminable. . . . One of the younger men said he counted two hundred and twenty cars. With the approaching darkness, and the smoke and shadows of the train, it was often difficult to see our friend. We had heard no human sounds, no screams, but would we have heard anything at all, with the racket of the train crossing overhead?

"When the last car began to curve around the mountain, we could just make out Félix's lonely figure still hanging beneath the bridge. We all watched in relief and amazement as he pulled himself up and at last finished walking, slowly and calmly, along the tracks to the other side of the gorge."

After I heard that story, I saw Félix Caballero in a

whole new light. He still remained as quiet as ever, prompting a smile from my mother and her sisters as he sat silently in his rocking chair. But in my mind's eye, I saw him crossing that treacherous bridge, stopping to think calmly of what to do to save his life, emerging all covered with soot and smoke but triumphantly alive—a lonely man, hanging under a railroad bridge at dusk, suspended from his surveyor's poles over a rocky gorge.

If there was so much courage, such an ability to calmly confront danger in the quiet, aging man who sat rocking in our living room, what other wonders might lie hidden in every human soul?

Lightning

Mario, my father's younger brother, was a teacher in the countryside. To get to his school he had to take the train and then ride for a few hours on horseback.

The school was housed in a *bohío,* a country hut made of royal palm boards and thatched with royal palm leaves. The students sat on benches, three, four, or when attendance was especially good, even five to a bench. But attendance was seldom good. In the countryside, girls often stayed home to help with their little brothers and sisters, to do the washing, and to gather wood for the stove. Boys often missed school because they had to help in the fields, planting, weeding, or harvesting. For the most part, the people did not believe that school would much improve their lives, and therefore they did not see a compelling reason to attend.

My uncle came back to the city every Friday night, tired, exhausted, and somewhat depressed. "What's the use?" I often heard him say. Soon he too cut class whenever possible.

Often, on Monday, he would procrastinate and miss the train. An upset stomach or a small cold was a reason not to travel. Many times he went on Tuesday, and the week would be only four days long. Other times he came back on Thursday night. "Attendance was poor this week," he would say. "It always gets worse on Friday, so I just came home."

My father never criticized him. Ever since their mother had died when my father was fifteen and my uncle only ten, my father had taken care of Mario. I think the painful memory of their shared loss, their unhappiness at having been sent to boarding school, the loneliness they had both felt, gave my father compassion for his brother. Although Mario was now a man, my father continued to indulge and protect him. My mother, on the other hand, constantly chided my uncle. "How are the children ever going to value their education, when you yourself don't? You could do so much for them. . . ."

My uncle was a person of few words. He drew back from arguments, and never tried to defend himself. In fact he seldom spoke much at all.

I could see my uncle's predicament. We were his

only family, and, I suspect, his only friends. It must have been hard to have my mother always reprimanding him, but he just kept silent, and continued to spend his weekends with us.

But one Friday night, Mario did not make his usual appearance at dinner. More surprisingly, he had still not returned by Saturday night, nor on Sunday. My mother asked my father, my father asked my grandfather, but no one seemed to know where he was.

Nor did we see or hear from him the following week. Everyone wondered and speculated and worried. There had been heavy rains, so maybe the rivers had flooded and he had been unable to get across. After all, he had often used this excuse in order to avoid going back to school on Monday. Perhaps this time it had really happened after all.

The next weekend arrived but there was still no news of my uncle. Although my father became increasingly alarmed, there was no telephone or telegraph that could reach the remote countryside where the school was.

Three weeks later, when Mario finally returned, he looked like a different man. His normally pink skin was tanned, and his carefully polished nails were now broken and dirty. He needed a haircut. But for the first time ever, he looked sunburned and strong.

He said nothing at all about his absence, and as if by agreement, no one else mentioned it either. We all sat down to lunch.

We were enjoying the black beans and rice, the sweet fried plantains, when I noticed on my uncle's wrist a dark yellow scab, where he normally wore his wristwatch.

"*Tío*, what is that?" I couldn't help but ask.

"Oh, that . . . it's from the lightning."

There was a moment of silence. My mother set down the pitcher of coconut water, even though her glass was still empty. My father put down his fork and knife. No one said a word. At last my uncle spoke.

"That first week I was gone," my uncle said slowly, "there was a very big storm." And then he stopped.

"And?" prompted my father. "What about the lightning?"

"The lightning was everywhere," my uncle continued. "It was difficult to teach above the noise of the thunder. The lightning bolts seemed to be flashing all around us. . . ." And then he stopped again.

"Were many children present?" my mother asked.

And as if this were the very cue he needed, my uncle resumed the story:

"Yes, for once, they were all present. It was crowded and hot in that small room. And the children were all excited, as if charged by the storm. And then, it happened. . . ."

We all held still, waiting to hear what came next.

"I didn't even hear the thunder when lightning struck the large mango tree next to the school. I simply passed out. When I awoke, I felt an intense pain in my arm. My watch had melted right on to my wrist. But I didn't pay attention to it. All of the children were strewn about the floor. Every single one of them..."

"Were they dead?" There was panic in my mother's voice.

"That's what I thought when I first saw them. 'Here they are all dead,' I said to myself. 'All because they came to hear a teacher who doesn't even believe in their future.' But little by little, they began to stir and to wake up. Thank goodness, no one was hurt. They weren't even scared. But I, I was. . . ."

"So that's why you didn't come all this time...," said my father, more to himself than to my uncle.

"I've been working on the school. I asked a couple of the fathers to help me enlarge it. And we are building some more benches. We also made a larger blackboard. It will take a while before everything is in place. I spoke with one of the families about renting a room, because I am turning my old room next to the classroom into an art workshop. There is so much to be done, I'll probably be coming back only once a month to get supplies."

My mother poured herself a large glass of coconut water. As she lifted it to her lips, a golden ray of light came in through the dining room window and lit up the glass. It looked as if she were making an offering.

Samoné

Dark clouds had covered the sky all day. I was sitting in the window seat of a large front window that reached almost to the floor, looking down the road and waiting for the rain. Would there be a storm with bolts of lightning? If so, I would not be allowed to go outside; but if it were a peaceful tropical rain, I would be able to put on my bathing suit and run outdoors through the courtyard, into the garden, under the trees. I loved to stand under their canopies and let the water drip down on me from their leaves. How fresh and fragrant the water was as it fell from the orange and the lemon trees!

Just then I saw the man approaching. He was tall and burly, with an unkempt beard, large, bushy eyebrows, and well-tanned, weathered skin. He had a burlap sack on his shoulder, and I was surprised to see him turn toward our house. When he knocked on the door I was scared. Instead of calling my mother or one of my aunts, I went in search of my father.

"I'm looking for work," were the man's first words. "And I can do anything . . . plant, weed, feed the chickens, tend the horses, milk the cows."

My father didn't reply. I knew we weren't looking for anyone. The hacienda was not a true farm anymore. We kept hardly any animals, and we certainly didn't need anyone to feed my grandmother's chickens and peacocks. But the man was determined to let us know all that he could do.

"I can make charcoal . . . and you seem to have plenty of *marabú.*" He was right. The thorny plant that could be converted into charcoal had taken over most of the fallow farmland.

"It won't cost you much. Just a place to stay and something to eat," he said, and then he looked at me. A broad smile lit his face. "And I know plenty of stories to tell the little girl. . . ."

I saw my father return his smile. He was not sure about needing to make charcoal, but he would find something for this man to do.

Samoné had spoken truly. Work seemed to be his life, and he was very good at everything he did. He was up before sunrise, and except for a brief pause for a cup of coffee and a quick lunch, he worked until sundown. Soon Samoné had become part of the family.

The farm began to show the fruits of his care. Where there had only been weeds before, now there was a vegetable garden. The hens seemed to lay more eggs, pleased with the fresh-cut grass he brought them from the river. There were more chicks, more geese.

But best of all, every evening after dinner, Samoné shared with us the one gift he had not mentioned, and music filled the air. He sat outside, leaning against a wall on a sturdy *taburete*, a rustic chair with cowhide back and seat, and played his accordion. Although his speaking voice was deep and strong, I never heard him sing. Instead, he would hum softly to himself as he played. It was the accordion that sang for him: sad, melancholy tangos, sweet boleros, lively polkas, enchanting habaneras.

Just as during the day he worked without pause, at night Samoné played without stopping. He played while my mother helped me undress and get into my pajamas, he played while my father told me bedtime stories, and he would still be playing as I lay quietly in bed, trying to not fall asleep so that I could continue listening as the music came in through my window, bathed in the fragrance of jasmine....

Samoné had been with us for a couple of years

when he again suggested that he make some charcoal. My father tried to dissuade him, saying that it was too much work and too dangerous, hardly worth the amount of effort it demanded. But Samoné was determined to start his own furnaces.

To make the coal, it was first necessary to cut *marabú* bushes, and then to strip the thorny branches until only the trunk remained, clean as a stick. These sticks were then propped up, as if to form a tepee. When several layers of sticks were in place, they were covered with dirt, leaving only a small opening through which to ignite the wood. The strong wood would burn slow and hot over a period of days, turning gradually into charcoal.

It was important that the charcoal maker watch the *horno*, the charcoal oven, day and night. Sometimes, if one had not been sealed correctly, it would burst into flames. Other times, if the green wood contained too much sap, it could explode.

Samoné, however, never got to guard his furnace. While he was cutting through the thorny *marabú* bushes, his machete got caught on a rebellious branch, slipped out of his hand, and came slashing down on his right arm.

It was almost Christmas when it happened. My mother and I had been decorating our small tree. I sat in the front window seat, alternately looking inside at the beautiful tree and outside at a group of boys who were flying kites in the open field across the road.

Suddenly Samoné staggered in and almost fell. He left a bright crimson trail behind him.

"Mother!" I screamed, grateful that she was so close at hand.

A passing car stopped to drive Samoné and my mother to the hospital. As they drove away, she held his arm still with towels that were already as red as carnations.

For weeks, only Samoné's burly fingers, purple and inflamed, poked out from his bandaged arm. Unable to work, Samoné himself walked around in a daze. The only thing that would liven him up a bit was bringing fresh grass to the hens. As he could only use one hand, even this simple task now took him most of the day.

I couldn't wait for the day that the bandage would come off. But when it was finally removed, and the ugly scar along his arm was laid bare, Samoné discovered that he could not get his hand to respond. He could not close his fingers, nor could they hold any weight.

My uncle gave Samoné a rubber ball and encouraged him to try to hold it in his hand, to try to close his fingers around it. It was heartbreaking to see the ball fall again and again. Samoné did not give up, and would sit on the porch for hours with the ball, but he looked embarrassed and ashamed as the ball continued to fall.

Since the accident, there had been no accordion music at night. Now that the bandages had come off, the nightly silence felt even more oppressive to me. I began to go to the river with Samoné to help him bring in the grass. Before, whenever we had spent time together, he had told me stories about bright rabbits and nasty foxes. Yet now all that I heard from him were heavy sighs. It was as though the purpose in his life had left him, drained out through the hand he could no longer use.

Then Samoné began to disappear in the afternoons. No one knew where he went. Nobody said much about it but I could see worried looks on my mother's face when he began to skip dinner too. Sometimes, when he was gone, I felt as though I heard an echo of his music.

Then one night, when I was already in bed, I did hear it. Somewhat tentative, and not as bright as it had been before, but there it was, the beautiful sound of a *guajira*, a gentle love song from the Cuban countryside. Samoné, practicing tenaciously in solitude, had found a way to create music again.

I jumped out of bed, tiptoed into the dining room, and looked out into the courtyard. There he was, poised somewhat awkwardly on his *taburete*, opening and closing the accordion with his knees while he played the keys with his left hand. Yet the music sounded soft and clear, accompanied by Samoné's familiar hum, while the rays of moonlight, filtering through the branches of the flame trees, shone upon the smile that lit his face.

The Legend

I have always loved legends and stories that relate mysterious events. There were many legends connected to our old house, the Quinta Simoni. People said that there was a buried treasure somewhere on the land, and that ghosts were seen at night trying to find it. Some swore that the spirits of former slaves could be heard crying at night. Others were convinced that they had seen the ghost of Ignacio Agramonte, the patriot from the Cuban War for Independence who had once lived in the house, riding his horse through the fields at night. We knew that what people mistook for a white horse was the white arch which stood far behind the house, in the abandoned garden next to the river. As for the other ghosts, we ourselves had never seen nor heard them. But on one occasion I actually had the chance to witness a legend being born, though at the time it happened I did not realize how enduring a legend it would be.

Our house stood on the outskirts of town, far away from any other house except for the tiny house where my great-grandmother lived. Across the road there was an empty field named Parque La Habana. Except for the name, it had none of the trappings of a park; it was just a vast and open stretch of land where cows occasionally grazed and where children came to fly their kites. At night, a few lights shone dimly on the stretch of road right in front of the house. Otherwise, the darkness was complete.

As the road curved out away from town, it came to the army headquarters. A little farther still, it reached a village of palm huts and simple shacks. To shorten their way to town, the people who lived in the village had cut some trails through the thorny *marabú* bushes that covered most of the neglected fields behind our house. But the trails through the fields were not only being used as a shortcut; a thief or thieves had begun to frequent the trails at night.

One night, a hen was stolen; the next, clothes from the clothes line, a spade, a bucket, or a wheelbarrow. Things were constantly disappearing, and each time it seemed as if the thief or thieves were becoming bolder.

The thieves had their big night after Día de Reyes, a feast celebrated on January 6 when children in Cuba receive their holiday gifts. My uncle Medardito's new watch, which he had placed upon his nightstand; my cousin Jorge's new bicycle; my own *carriola,* the scooter that I had longed for, had all disappeared by the morning after the holiday.

"This is too much," the family agreed. "Things have gone too far."

"We need to put a stop to the thievery," said my uncle.

"But what can we do?" asked one of my aunts.

"I have an idea," proposed my father. His plan was that my uncle and he walk down the trails toward the village in the middle of the night. Halfway there, they would shoot some shots from the revolver into the air. "Maybe that will frighten the thieves away, by letting them know that we are armed."

Over the next few days, I heard repeated accounts of the events that were set in motion by my father's plan. My uncle and he had indeed set out that night. As they began to walk toward the village, Samoné, our hired hand, decided to join them.

The three of them made their way with a flashlight, not always succeeding at steering clear of the thornbushes. When they were halfway to the village, my father pulled out his gun and shot some blanks into the air. To his surprise, Samoné began screaming in a convincing imitation of a woman's voice: "Please, don't kill me! Don't kill me, please, I beg of you!"

My uncle then took up the cue, shouting: "Oh yes, I will! Prepare to die!"

He then signaled to my father to shoot again. Meanwhile, my father was completely dismayed. This was not at all what he had had in mind; but he followed my uncle's suggestion and shot a few more blanks, which were accompanied by Samoné's piercing scream.

Then the three hurriedly returned to the house, my uncle and Samoné patting each other on the back and barely restraining their laughter, my father quite angry at both of them.

"You're nothing but a bunch of clowns," he told them when they arrived back at the courtyard. And he stalked off to bed, leaving the other two men to rejoice in their prank.

It was well past midnight when we heard insistent knocks at our door. Someone was pounding the hand-shaped brass knocker with all his might. The lights came on, and my father opened the door, with all of us looking on, half-asleep in our pajamas and nightgowns.

A group of men from the village had gathered outside, carrying flashlights and torches. Some were armed with revolvers, others with machetes.

"Didn't you hear anything?" one of them asked.

"A woman has been killed. You must have heard the shots."

"Were those shots?" My father feigned surprise.

"We thought it was thunder," volunteered my mother.

"We must go find the body," insisted one of the men. "Won't you come with us?" Somehow his words sounded more like a threat than an invitation.

My father and uncle rushed to get dressed and accompany the men. Who knew how the armed men would react if they learned that what they had heard was only a prank.

The men searched the fields throughout the night, and for several days afterwards. They crisscrossed the *marabú* fields, cutting new trails with their machetes. It was when they at last decided that the woman's body would not be found that the legend was born.

A few months after all this took place, we moved from the big house to the city. We lived in the city for several years, until my father decided to open a road in the fields behind where the big house still stood and build a smaller house next to the river. When he looked to hire some people from the village to clear the land, none of the local people were willing to do it. "It's a holy place," they said. "That land is sacred."

My father finally gave up trying to convince the villagers, and instead brought in workers from the other side of town. Most of the land had already been cleared when the surprised workers found, in the very center of the *marabú* fields, mounds of objects commonly used as offerings: red ribbons, jars filled with American pennies, remains of sacrificial roosters. . . . Always respectful of other people's beliefs, my father asked the workers to leave that area untouched, although he well knew the origin of the "sacredness" of the place.

More than twenty years later, I had the opportunity to visit my homeland again, and journey to this site of my childhood. The fields behind the house had changed greatly in those twenty years. They had been parceled into lots, and houses had been built. No sign remained of the *marabú* thickets.

I went to visit the family of our former caretakers. They had come to work for us from another region after the small house had been built, and knew nothing of the old prank.

Emilio, the father, invited me happily into his home. There in the living room stood a large altar. Flowers, candles, offerings of fruit, and statues of many different saints formed a colorful pyramid.

"Did you know that this is holy land, my child?" Emilio asked, disregarding the fact that my hair was already turning gray. "You see, many years ago, a saintly woman lived in this area. She was killed when she refused to accept a man's advances. Since her body was holy, it disappeared and was never found. From that time on, her memory has been revered. . . ."

I nodded and said nothing, accepting in his faith in this fictitious woman the reverence deserved by all women, and the remembrance merited by the countless number of human beings who have indeed been victimized. Although I know the truth, the validity of his faith was for no one to question.

Then I followed Emilio to the backyard, where he proudly showed me his fruit trees: mangoes, *guayabos,* cherimoyas, *anones.*

"But Emilio," I asked, amazed, "wasn't all this an old stretch of dry riverbed? And wasn't there a steep ravine right behind your house?"

"I filled it in myself," Emilio said proudly. "For years, I wouldn't let myself go to bed without bringing a few buckets of earth to empty into the gully." My eyes wandered slowly over the trees that he, with incredible patience, had been able to plant by first filling in, a little bit every year, the old dry bed of the river. And it was then that I realized that this land, painstakingly built up bucket by bucket, was, indeed, truly sacred land, blessed by the miracle of human faith and perseverance.

Canelo

The rain had barely stopped. I was ready to ask my mother permission to go out and play when I saw the dog, a thinner dog than I'd ever seen before. His ribs seemed about to break through the skin. He had lost whole patches of hair and he looked as if he had just been rolling in the ashes of a campfire. But the saddest thing was to see him drag his hind leg, which hung black and lifeless as a piece of burned wood.

"Daddy, help him! Help him!" I cried as I went looking for my father. "Please, help him get well again."

My mother, my aunts, and my uncle all rushed out to see why I was crying.

"Don't get close!" someone warned. "That dog is sick!"

"Poor animal! The only kind thing to do is to put him out of his misery."

"Yes. Let's put an end to his suffering," agreed another.

But I kept crying: "Help him, Daddy. Please, help him." And my father, giving my hand a tight squeeze for reassurance, promised: "We'll help him get well."

Healing the dog was not a simple matter. My father brought some rope and tied it around his neck. The dog let himself be led by the rope, perhaps calmed by my father's soothing voice or maybe just too exhausted to be able to protest.

My father tied him to the thick trunk of a *caimito* tree, behind the old coach house that stood halfway down the lane bordered by the flame trees. He covered the dog's body with a mixture of oil and sulfur. The small dog trembled but remained silent. The flies flew away, and now his broken leg was not black but gray and red instead.

"He has gangrene," said my father with a serious note in his voice. "He'll live only if I amputate his leg."

My mother brought cotton, rags, gauze, and a dark bottle. The rags soaked in chloroform put the dog to sleep. My father cut off the gangrenous leg with great precision, as if he were a surgeon instead of a surveyor, and carefully bandaged the stub.

"Now it's all a matter of whether he tears the bandage apart, or whether he allows the wound to heal," he said as he went off to disinfect his hands.

Never had there been a more cooperative patient. The small dog did not even attempt to touch the bandage.

In fact he hardly moved at all, barely changing his position under the tree, and moving only as much as he needed to, in order to remain in the shade. He only perked up when my father placed a half gourd filled with food scraps from the table in front of him.

I was forbidden to go near the dog. Filled with both compassion and fear, I watched him from a distance. I would bring my doll to visit him, and I would play the solitary games of an only child as close as I was allowed to come.

As the dog lay on the *caimito* leaves, he would watch me skip rope, or hop on one foot on the silhouette of a snail that I had traced with a stick in the soft earth. Little by little, his fur grew back in the bald patches. And soon his ribs were not so visible anymore. When my father finally took off the bandages, I was happy to see that the leg stub had healed.

By then, we had been calling him Canelo. And everyone took it for granted that he would stay with us.

Once he was no longer confined by the rope, Canelo would follow me, but he always kept his distance. He would keep me company, but never come close, just as I had kept him company from a distance while he was healing.

But with my father—what a difference! Every day, as soon as my father got off the bus at the bus stop across the road, Canelo would come running, from the farthest corner of the farm, as if instead of three legs, he had them all; and all the while he would wave his tail as fast as a bongo player drumming a rumba.

The Rag Dolls

My great-grandmother Mina was tiny, as time not only wrinkled but also shrunk her. She was not very much taller than the jasmine and the rose bushes she tended in her garden in the little house next to ours. Like the raisins she sprinkled generously in our *arroz con leche*, the rice pudding she made that smelled of cinnamon and cloves, her wrinkled form was filled with sweetness.

When she was not in the kitchen or in the garden, she would often sit in a rocking chair and sew. In her hands scraps of cloth became multicolored quilts of various sizes. The large ones were wedding gifts for her many granddaughters; the small ones, greeting gifts for new great-grandchildren.

Yet the best pieces of cloth she saved for her rag

dolls. As the light left her eyes and they became covered with an opaque glaze, she spent less and less time in the kitchen and the garden. Unable to see, she could not stitch together the scraps and patches, so she stopped making quilts and took to crochet. But her blindness did not prevent her from making dolls. Her fingers, which had created dolls for so long, were able to give shape to the dolls' heads, to braid wool for their hair, to form their bodies and limbs.

Because she could not see the colors, I would help separate the greens and blues and reds that would become long skirts and bright head scarves. She would ask me: "This soft velvety piece, is it black? Can you find me a nice dark brown? A creamy chocolate? A toasted almond? A bright cinnamon?" And so the dolls would receive faces that resembled those of the neighborhood children.

Once a week her sister Genoveva came to visit from the other end of town, and on each doll she would embroider the dark round eyes, the lips, the two dots for a nose.

The dolls sat on the windowsill, four, five, six at a time. Little girls—some carrying cans full of water that their mothers needed to do the laundry, others loaded down with a bag of coal for cooking, and pulling a reluctant little brother or sister by the hand—would take a quick look to see whether the dolls had changed from the previous week. Or maybe, late in the afternoon, free of chores, skipping on one foot, jumping with a frayed rope, they would glance in the direction of the window and smile.

Whenever birthdays approached, mothers came knocking at Mina's door, in their hands an old handkerchief with coins tied up in a corner. "How much for the one with the red skirt?" they would ask. "And for the pretty one with the braids?"

Sunken in her rocking chair, my great-grandmother, sightless, knew. She knew when to say twenty-five cents, thirty, forty, to honor the woman's pride, to allow her the joy of giving. She also knew when to say, "I'd like so much for Marisa to have it. Seven she'll be, won't she?" and hand it to the mother saying, "Just save me some scraps, I'll make another one. . . ."

At other times, a young mother, weathered down by long hours of laundering and boiling clothes under the sun, of cooking in makeshift stoves made of old lard cans, would come to my grandmother's house, saying only, "I've brought you a few oranges, or mangoes, or some watercress . . ." and my great-grandmother would close her sightless eyes a moment, concentrating, before saying, "Oh yes, Manuelita will be five very soon now, won't she? Isn't it time she had her own doll? Do you see any she would like?" The mother's hand would go up to her face, to cover a bashful smile. And the doll would leave its place on the front window, wrapped in the old newspaper that had previously held the golden, red, green offerings.

Mathematics

M y great-grandmother Mina never went to school. She never learned to read or write. And she never studied the multiplication tables.

When she heard me trying to memorize three times three equals nine, three times four equals twelve, she'd say, "My sweet God, child, what are you doing? Becoming like my Cotita?" Cotita was her green parrot, which perched on a metal ring in her kitchen.

As she grew older and more frail, Mina spent most of her days in bed. She had borne five daughters and a son before my great-grandfather had abandoned her. As fate would have it, their lives turned out very differently. Two children became landowners, like their father before them; two lived in extreme poverty; while the other two were comfortable if not rich. And as each of those six children had his or her own children, the diversity in their lives became even greater. But they all had in common their love for the little weathered woman who lived simply in the poor, tiny house next to ours, with her seventh child, a son born much later to a different father.

All of her children, rich and poor, dropped by to see her often. And because there were so many grandchildren and great-grandchildren, someone would come by to visit every day. Seldom did they come with empty hands; and the gifts they brought reflected the means of the giver.

My great-grandmother Mina greeted each one of her visitors as if he or she were the most important person in the world to her, which at that moment was undoubtedly true. She shared jokes, always remembering who had told her the joke in the first place. And she'd tell the visitor the latest news about everyone in the family. So although the children had drifted apart, following their own paths, she remained a constant link between them. But mainly she listened, somehow drawing from each visitor that which was truly important to hear.

Mina received the presents that were offered her with great joy and a mischievous smile. She was as pleased by a bunch of wildflowers or an orange as she was by a pair of slippers, a shawl, or a set of towels. She would then point to her closet. "On the second shelf," she would say, "to the left," with precise instructions, as if her blind eyes could still see, "there's a can of peaches." Or she'd explain,

"In the top drawer, to the right, there's a box of handkerchiefs."

And in this way, the poor granddaughter who came in with a few oranges would go home with a new pair of socks. The tired daughter who brought a jar of homemade guava jelly would leave with a scarf or with an envelope that would help meet the rent payment. And the rich son would receive the gift of an orange. All were given with the greatest simplicity, and with utmost joy.

My great-grandmother Mina, who never went to school, who could not read and never learned the multiplication tables, but who remembered the birth date and the exact age of seven children, thirty-four grandchildren, seventy-five great grandchildren, and a few great great-grandchildren, knew a different kind of mathematics from the heartless tables I learned by rote. She knew how to add and subtract, how to accept and to give and to share so that the balance was always one of love.

The Ice-Cream Man

∞

At home they kept reminding us of the war, World War II, especially during meals. "Before the war," my parents and aunts would say, "there was plenty of butter. Now we have to make our own."

My mother would save the cream that gathered at the top whenever she boiled fresh milk, adding a little more each day to the jar stored in the refrigerator. Once a week, she let me beat the cream into butter with a wooden spoon in a big bowl. When my arms began to ache, she would wash the butter with ice water in order to separate the curd from the whey. The butter we made was white, not yellow, but to me it tasted fresh and wonderful. I didn't know or miss any other kind, nor did I believe, no matter what they said, that any butter could taste better than what we had.

The adults also complained of the lack of white sugar, "so abundant," they would say, "before the war." Yet I loved the coarse brown sugar we had. Many days for an afternoon snack, my mother would pinch a hole in a roll and fill it with brown sugar. I thought it was quite a treat.

The war was far away and distant, an empty word for a girl who loved homemade butter and brown sugar, and thought that it was fun to collect the aluminum wrappers from the occasional chocolate kiss my aunts would bring home from the movies.

Another complaint my mother and aunts had—the lack of cosmetics and nylon stockings—meant even less to me. And as for saving the slivers of soap—the fragrant soaps we used in the bathroom, the coarse yellow soap used for washing clothes and dishes—I found it all fun. The remnants were melted together in a tin can, yielding a multicolored, multipurpose bar in the shape of the can. To this day, I remember the smell of boiling soap, and collect tiny bars from hotels I visit in memory of those early years.

Although the shortages of things like butter and soap during the war didn't bother me, war showed its true ugly face to me in school. I was attending St. Paul's Episcopal School, one of the two American schools that at the time existed in my town. We wore a uniform of a sickly mustard color and were teased mercilessly by the children of the two nearby Catholic schools. But our parents were pleased that we had the opportunity to learn English and to be educated bilingually, so there we went. For days our teachers had promised that they were going to give us some free comic books to take home. We couldn't wait to receive them. Comics, which usually appeared only in the Sunday paper, were a treat that we waited for all week long. A whole book of comics for our very own seemed so special that it was hard to imagine. But when at last the long-awaited day came, what we were given was not very funny at all.

Some of my friends were hoping for comic books of Blondie, others wanted Donald Duck or Mickey Mouse, some of the boys looked forward to Tarzan or cowboy stories. Secretly, I was hoping for Prince Valiant. But instead of the type of comic book characters that we knew so well from the newspaper, these comic books depicted the fighting in the Pacific Ocean. In them the Japanese were shown as short, monsterlike creatures, painted a bright yellow, with unnaturally slanted eyes that made their faces look like fierce masks.

I had only met one Japanese person in my life. He was indeed small, even to my child's eyes, but he was not yellow, and his almond-shaped eyes looked bright and calm. He pushed an old ice-cream cart throughout the city, visiting a different neighborhood each day, as if to give everyone a chance to taste the delicious flavors of his ice cream: pineapple, coconut, cherimoya, and more.

My parents did not usually allow me to eat anything sold by the many vendors on the streets. "It's made with unclean water. You can get terrible diseases from unclean water," my father would say, in a tone that allowed no arguments. But they always let me buy ice cream from the Japanese man. "He boils the water," my mother knew. "He makes sure that his food is clean."

The Japanese man's ice cream was different from any other ice cream sold in stores or restaurants. It was lighter, and instead of the heavy, sugary taste so prevalent in Cuban desserts, it possessed only the natural sweetness of the fruits themselves. To me it seemed as if the essence of the fruit had magically become light and cold, without ceasing to be fruit.

The Japanese man served his ice cream differently too. For him it was almost an art. Instead of filling a little paper cup, or plopping a scoop of ice cream on a cone, he would spread it on a thick waffle, gently and evenly with a spatula. Then he covered it with another waffle, creating a thick ice-cream sandwich that sold for a nickel.

For those who could not afford to spend a whole nickel on ice cream, he had little waffle boats. The larger ones sold for two cents apiece, while the smaller ones were a penny. In these he packed the ice cream carefully too, filling the delicate boat to the brim, and then adding an extra dollop on top.

But often even a penny was too much for many of the children in my town. For every child who was able to purchase ice cream, there were two or three onlookers eyeing the meticulous process carefully, wishing that they too could taste the cool fresh coconut, banana, or guava.

The ice-cream man would take a quick glance around to make sure no adults were watching, that his next act of kindness would go unseen. And then he would lift the top of the wooden box in the front of the cart, where the waffles were kept, dig into a corner, and pull out some pieces of broken waffle. He would spread a dab of ice cream on each piece, and silently hand one to each of the hopeful children, with merely a hint of a soft smile on his face. Then he would close the lid and continue pushing the old cart along the streets.

He never yelled *"Helado! Heladeeero!"* like the other raucous ice-cream vendors did. He did not ring a bell nor blow a whistle. Yet somehow we always knew when he was in the neighborhood.

After I looked through the comic books I had been given to take home, the comic books that showed the hideous yellow faces, I tore each one to pieces, page by page, feeling sadness and great shame. How could it be, I wondered, that people could hate one another so much that they would want to fight and kill each other? I wanted no one else to see the little yellow monsters, because in my short years I had already met a real Japanese person, and he had brought a fresh and fragrant kindness, to the streets of my small town.

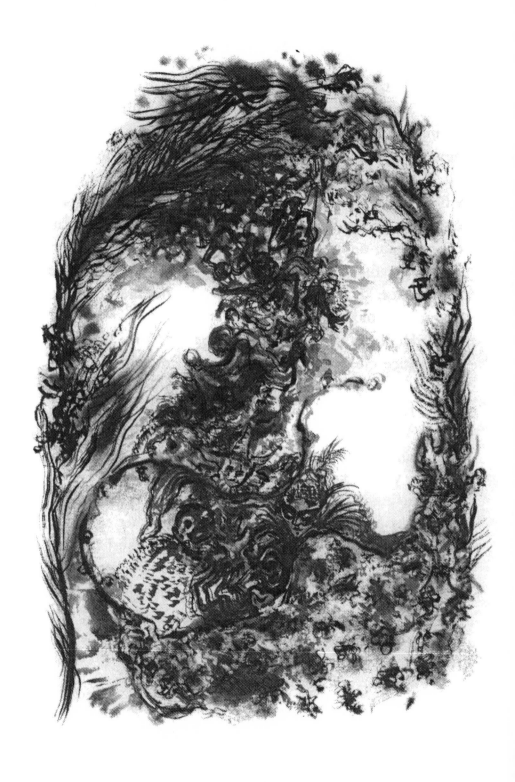

The Feast of San Juan

⚭

"¡*Mono viejo! Frijolito!*" "Old monkey! Little bean!" taunted a group of boys. They followed the man dressed in an outfit of flowered cloth that covered all of his body, except for holes for his eyes and mouth.

Hearing the boys' cries, the *mono viejo* turned around. The hundreds of bells that covered his suit filled the street with a jingling sound while he threatened the children with his thick tail, a long piece of heavy rope, also covered by the flowered cloth and by heavier, larger bells.

The children scattered, screaming, each running in a different direction, seeking refuge on porches and among the narrow crooked alleys. The *mono viejo* continued to jump and somersault with his pranks and antics throughout the streets of the town until another group of children gathered the courage to cry out: *"¡Mono viejo! Frijolito!"*

It was the Feast of San Juan (or Saint John), carnival time in Camagüey, which lasted throughout the month of June, and ended on the twenty-ninth. In Cuba, as in much of Spain and Latin America, each town celebrated the feast of the town on its own special day, depending on the town's patron saint. In Camagüey, the saint was for San Juan and the day June 24. But since June 29 was a very special day too, the Feast of Saint Peter and Saint Paul in the Catholic tradition, and it was only five days away, the Feast of San Juan got extended to that date.

By the first week of June, the face of the town had started to change. The brick and mortar of the town's walls began magically to blossom. Each neighborhood competed to be the best decorated. Triumphal arches made of palm leaves and flame tree branches in full bloom appeared everywhere. In some neighborhoods, young boys stretched a rope across the street to stop passing cars and ask for donations to decorate the neighborhood. In other areas of town the ardent flame tree branches and palms' greenery gave way to paper flowers and colored lights.

During the Feast of San Juan, all the social rules disappeared. In a town where everyone knew everyone else, where social codes were rigid and strict, and where no action passed unnoticed or unmentioned, everything was allowed during this month of the year. Men could dress as women, and everyone could follow his or her fancy to be a pirate or a princess, a courtly lady or a page, Superman or Tarzan, harlequin or queen. It was common for pale-skinned people to choose to wear black faces for Carnival, for once acknowledging their hidden and denied African heritage. Those who did not have a favorite fantasy and whose only goal was to have fun become *mamarrachos*. To be one all you needed to do was to disguise any identifiable feature. And so hair disappeared behind a stocking, hands inside a pair of socks, faces behind masks or perhaps behind fake noses and makeup. Anything worked as long as no one, not even the *mamarracho's* own mother could recognize him or her. Now, by changing their voices, the *mamarrachos* could appear at the homes of neighbors and friends, laugh and joke with every passerby, flirt with respectable matrons, make fun of the solemn members of the Professional Society—those who could add the title "doctor" before their name and sat pompously at their exclusive club.

At night, parades of floats followed, prescribed routes through the central streets of town, followed by horse-drawn carriages brought in by railroad from all over the island especially for the occasion. Flatbed trucks also joined the parade, carrying noisy groups of revelers who threw confetti and streamers to the people who filled the streets.

The parade became even livelier when the *comparsas* appeared—groups of twenty, forty, or sixty men and women, in matching costumes, and carrying *farolas,* long, decorated poles with lanterns on top. As the *comparsas* went by, moving as one in intricate dances, the people on the sidewalks, in doorways, and at windows all danced to their rhythm too, letting themselves be carried away by the music. As they moved their shoulders, waists, hips to the rhythm, they would sing along:

Mírala, ¡qué linda viene!	Look, how beautiful it comes!
Mírala, ¡qué linda va!	Look, how beautiful it goes!
La comparsa "Maravillas":	The *comparsa* "Many wonders"
que se va y no vuelve más.	leaves and will return no more.

More floats, carriages, and decorated trucks full of costumed people would come, and then another *comparsa*. Arms in ruffled sleeves held the tall *farolas* high, and everyone, those in the *comparsa* and on the sidewalk, men and women, parents and children, grandparents and grandchildren, would sing:

Al Carnaval de Oriente	I won't go off to Oriente for
no voy.	Carnival.
En Camagüey, ¡se goza mejor!	In Camagüey, we have it all!

At long last the parade would near its end . . . but what an end it was! It was time now for congas. Rolling their bodies to the rhythm of the bongos and the *tumbadoras*, the congas now appeared. Large groups of people, dancing together, but not in choreographic lines like the *comparsas*, just together. The first to arrive might resemble the preceding *comparsas*. Their rhythmic music had a melody that could be sung:

Uno, dos y tres	One, two, three
que paso más chévere	what a joyful step
que paso más chévere	what a joyful step
el de mi conga es.	of my conga roll.
Al tambor mayor delante	The head drum that leads
nadie lo puede igualar	the drumming has no equal to its beat
con el ritmo fascinante	for you see it has the rhythm
de mi Cuba tropical.	of my Cuban island heat.

But very soon, all resemblance to the more orderly *comparsas* disappeared. What coursed through the street was clearly the energy of the people. Perhaps there still remained a bongo, or a *tumbadora* drum, but now what predominated was the persistent rhythm, hypnotic and alluring, of steel against steel—old car wheels that had been turned into drums, struck with an iron rod.

As the majestic river flooded the streets with its powerful rhythms, everything that had appeared before became mere prelude. The courtly ladies with powdered wigs, the queen and her attendants, the harlequins, the false strength of make-believe supermen, all vanished, as the streets surrendered to the memory of jungles and of rivers, of ancestral rites of hunting, planting, and mating, rites once forgotten and still very much alive in the blood that now pounded to the accelerated beat of the congas. Blood that will never again be mine alone, but instead ours, blood that courses not only through my veins, but through all of us as one, as it reconnects with its roots— these powerful, vigorous African roots, once shamefully enslaved, now free, redeemed by the power of this driving rhythm, free and to be honored, now and for all time.

Epilogue

As a child of the countryside and the open air, our move to the town was difficult for me. Like a plant transplanted into too small a pot, lacking sunshine and rain, I withered. But as the congas rolled along the streets of the town, I—half-hidden behind the door, fearful of the strength of the drums—woke up to the echo of their rhythm in my blood.

As I watched the crowd, growing from several dozen people to a couple of hundred, beating their drums, whether of hide or steel, I realized that my own roots went very far indeed.

Some of them came from Spain, when my grandfather Modesto hid as a stowaway on a ship or when my grandfather Medardo left because he couldn't marry the cousin he loved. But my roots also went deep into the

Cuban soil, to the *siboneyes* whose voices sound in the names of my town, Camagüey, of the river of my childhood, Tínima, and whose indomitable spirit remains in the proud royal palms. And my roots also reach far back to Africa, to the land where rhythms were captured by the drums, the land where the majestic ceibas send their sacred branches up toward the sky.

While these roots nourished me, the trunks that grew up from them invited me to climb high, to watch the world from the vantage point of their branches.

My father once built me a tree house up in the branches of an algaroba tree growing by the river. From that hideout, if I stayed as quiet as the herons, I could watch the turtles come out to bask in the sun on the rocks, the frogs leap to catch flies, and the fish shine under the water. The whole world of the river was right there for me to take in.

From the security of my home, I could also observe the world around me: the street vendors, the beggars, the people on the street—each one with their own life, each one with a story of their own to tell.

As I write these lines, fall is arriving to the mountains of northern California where I now live. As the foliage turns bright yellow and deep red, I absorb its powerful colors. Occasionally one leaf will catch my attention, perhaps because its shape is so perfect, or its color so intense—and so I pick it up, and bring it inside. And it is as though with that one leaf, I have somehow brought the whole forest to my desk.

And so these stories. There are still many more of them hanging in the branches of the trees of my childhood. I have picked up a few, hoping to give you a taste of those bygone days sweetened by mangoes and guavas, perfumed by the fragrance of orange blossoms, brightened by the blooming branches of the flame trees.

CPSIA information can be obtained at www.ICGtesting.com
Printed in the USA
LVOW122133281012

304816LV00003B/2/A